Communicate!

Animal Talk

Dona Herweck Rice

Publishing Credits

Rachelle Cracchiolo, M.S.Ed., *Publisher*
Conni Medina, M.A.Ed., *Managing Editor*
Nika Fabienke, Ed.D., *Series Developer*
June Kikuchi, *Content Director*
John Leach, *Assistant Editor*
Kevin Pham, *Graphic Designer*

TIME For Kids and the TIME For Kids logo are registered trademarks of TIME Inc. Used under license.

Image Credits: All images from iStock and/or Shutterstock.

Library of Congress Cataloging-in-Publication Data

Names: Rice, Dona, author.
Title: Communicate : animal talk / Dona Herweck Rice.
Description: Huntington Beach, CA : Teacher Created Materials, [2018] |
    Audience: K to Grade 3.
Identifiers: LCCN 2017029997 (print) | LCCN 2017031772 (ebook) | ISBN
    9781425853235 (eBook) | ISBN 9781425849498 (pbk.)
Subjects: LCSH: Animal communication--Juvenile literature.
Classification: LCC QL776 (ebook) | LCC QL776 .R53 2018 (print) | DDC
    591.59--dc23
LC record available at https://lccn.loc.gov/2017029997

Teacher Created Materials
5301 Oceanus Drive
Huntington Beach, CA 92649-1030
http://www.tcmpub.com
ISBN 978-1-4258-4949-8
© 2018 Teacher Created Materials, Inc.
Printed in China
Nordica.072018.CA21800723

Animals use their bodies to talk.

Elephants talk with their trunks.

They touch.

Dogs talk with their tails.

They wag.

Crabs talk with their claws.

They wave.

Bees talk with their bodies.

They dance.

Animals talk in many ways.